Short Story Study Journal

for GCSE/ International GCSE English Literature

*A place to record your ideas
and observations*

Copyright © 2020 Dorothy Murphy

All rights reserved. Please do not scan or copy any part of this book in any form without written permission from me, unless you are a reviewer, who may quote brief passages in a review.

Jacket design by Jamie Stewart.
Cover image by Pawel Czerwinski (unsplash.com)

ISBN: 9798657448634

This book belongs to

Name ....

Address ....

....

....

Date ....

Acknowledgements

Thank you...

...to Jamie Stewart, who did a painstakingly careful job of the design

...to Darcy Baldwin at DJB Fonts

...and to the home educating community of the UK

Contents

Welcome! 1
How to use this book 1

Preparing for your Literature exam short story question 3
    The study process 4
    Ask yourself some questions 4
    Revision 5
    Writing in the exam 5
    Responding to the question 6
    Introductions and conclusions 7
    Story arcs 9

Story 1 11
    Reaction 11
    Story arc 12
    Context 13
    Themes 14
    Point 14
    Characters 15
    Character quotes 17
    Anything unusual/ surprising 18
    Turning point 18
    Ending 18
    Language 19
    Mood/ tone/ atmosphere 20
    Other significant quotes 21
    Essay questions 22
    Homework 23

Contents

Story 2 25

Story 3 39

Story 4 53

Story 5 67

Story 6 81

Story 7 95

Story 8 109

Story 9 123

Story 10 137

About the author 151

Welcome!

This is **your** study journal. It is where you can write your own observations and record your discoveries about the collection of short stories you are required to study as part of your GCSE/ International GSCE.

I want to encourage you to believe that your own thoughts are important and valuable. Don't listen to that inner voice that may be telling you that your ideas don't matter and you need to reproduce other people's ideas in the exam!

How to use this book

First, write **your name** in the front. The book is yours! Add your address and the date if you want to.

There is space for you to write about 10 short stories in total. Write the **title of each story** in the Contents pages of this journal so that you can easily look up each story.

In each section,
- there is a space to write the **title** and **author**
- there are several pages of journal prompts (questions) to help guide you as you engage with each story
- there is enough space to keep adding more discoveries and observations throughout your period of study

Good luck and enjoy your time exploring every single story.

Dorothy Murphy
Oxford
Summer 2020

Preparing for your GCSE/ International GCSE Literature Exam
Short Story Question

As part of your Literature GCSE/ International GCSE exam, you may be studying a collection of short stories instead of a novel. Check your exam specification for exactly which ones. You will need to study each one separately, think about it and develop an authentically **personal response** to it.

Some people are nervous about studying Literature for themselves and place too much reliance on what other people tell them to think about the things they are reading. Your own ideas are just as valid!

Don't simply memorise other people's ideas and regurgitate them in the exam. In fact, this can, and often does, result in a poor grade. Examiners can tell when a candidate does not understand what they are reading and writing.

Don't worry! You can do this!

Here is a possible process for working on each short story in turn, and developing a personal response, which might be helpful for you. You can use this journal as a place to keep all your thoughts and discoveries.

The study process

- **Read** the story. Most people will catch more detail if they read it aloud to themselves or someone else.
- When you finish, think about your **immediate reactions** to the story. Jot them down on the first of the pages dedicated to that story.
- **Find out** something about the **author**. Where and in what historical context were they writing?
- Without looking at what other people have written about the story, think about **your own response** to it. What do you think the author is trying to communicate to you?
- **Record** your observations in this journal under the various prompt questions.

Ask yourself some questions as you are reading

- Are you enjoying reading the story? If so, why? If not, why not?
- Are any of the characters interesting or memorable?
- Is there an obvious protagonist (hero/ heroine, the person around whom the plot revolves)?
- What are the important themes?
- Is the author trying to make any kind of point? If so, what is it?
- Is there a section which is particularly dramatic? Surprising? Moving?
- Is the ending satisfying to you?
- What questions would you like to ask the author if you could?

Through asking yourself these questions about the story and recording your ideas in the following pages, you will be able to develop a written response to it.

All these notes will help you when you begin to practise writing essays.

Revision

Use this book to help you revise as the exam approaches. The best revision for the prose question in the exam is to read the stories again. Then, read your notes and see if you still agree with what you have written. Perhaps you have alternative or additional ideas to write in the boxes? It may help to write your new ideas in a different colour.

Writing in the exam

The skill of writing about literature is that it should be…

> **an informed, personal response
> with close reference to the text.**

'Informed'
This is partly to do with understanding the effect of the context of the story. It is not necessary or desirable to have done lots of research on the writer's life and times, but some facts may be helpful to you as you work to understand the story. Evaluating the importance of the information you discover will be part of the process of your studies.

Part of being 'informed' also means understanding the craft of the author. But beware of simply 'device spotting' and flitting from one comment about onomatopoeia, for example, to another. Yes, you need to be able to recognise that a writer has used imagery, for example, but it is much more important to be able to confidently explain what effect it has on the reader. (That's you, not your teacher, by the way!)

Don't fall into the trap of approaching the exam question on one of these short stories in the same way as you would a piece of text in the Unseen Poetry and Prose part of the exam, if you are taking that option. The examiners will expect you to have thoroughly **studied** the collection of stories in advance and the quality of your response will need to reflect that.

'Personal'

Answering a question in an exam is an invitation to articulate **your own**, authentically personal, response to the story. If all you do is reiterate someone else's response (something you've read somewhere or what someone has told you to write) then the response will not be personal. The examiner will be able to tell that and start to doubt whether you have an understanding of the story or have even read it before the exam.

'Close reference to the text'

This means quoting from the story in your essay to illustrate your argument, or referring to a specific detail regarding language or structure, for example. Short quotes are much better than long ones. When you focus on 2-3 words, you are showing specifically what you mean. When you quote 2-3 lines, the examiner may suspect that you are simply filling in space because you cannot answer the question properly.

Responding to the question

It can be very tempting to try to answer a question you wish you had been asked. This applies to any exam. Avoid this common error. In order to fully focus on answering the question right there in front of you in the exam, make sure you read it carefully and closely and that you take note of any key words in it. Do this, using a highlighter, and annotate the question if it helps.

Let's say the question is this - (I have highlighted the key words **in bold** for you here):

'**How** does the author make this such a **tense** (or moving or hilarious or tragic) **moment** in the story?'

The word '*how*' expects an exploration of the author's techniques, but this analysis always sits within the context of the rest of the short story. You need to understand the whole story to be able to thoroughly answer the question of '*how*' the writer has created such a tense moment '*in the story*'. It may be a pivotal moment in the plot or in the development of a character. This question is not the same as an 'unseen' question, where you may not be familiar with the whole text.

Another possible question:

'**How** is the theme of **sacrifice developed** during the course of this story?'

The word '*how*' requires detailed evidence relating to the way the author developed the theme. The theme here is '*sacrifice*', not another theme you may have noticed. Focus on that! It's asking about the development, too. Does the author change their mind about the theme? Does the idea of sacrifice change at all? Does your response to the idea of sacrifice change?

Introductions and conclusions

Lengthy, vague introductions and repetitive conclusions are both unnecessary and pointless. Spend all your available time planning and writing an answer which begins to respond to the question in the very first sentence and continues to build an argument supported by frequent, embedded quotations. 'Embedded' just means they flow naturally throughout your essay.

Your eventual answer in the exam depends and rests on the work you do before the exam. In studying, reflecting on and practising writing about the story you will be preparing to give an excellent...

**informed, personal response
with close reference to the text.**

Happy studying!

Dorothy

A word about Story Arcs

Stories have a story arc (or narrative arc), which is the structure or shape of the story, made up of the events. There is usually a building of tension towards a climax. They may often be visualised in a quick diagram.

Here are a few examples:

```
                                    Climax
                      Conflict or           Resolution
                      challenge
Setting   Intro to
          characters
```

Some stories start at the moment of highest tension and then go back to the beginning to explain how things reached that point.

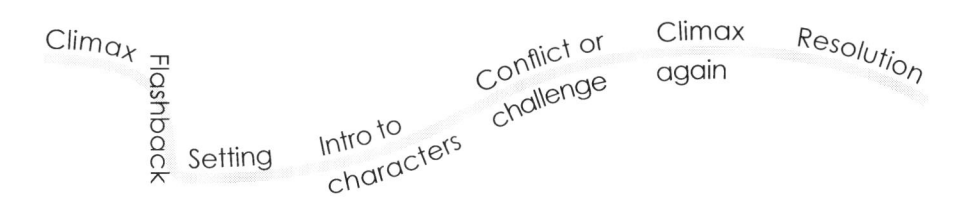

```
Climax                              Climax
     Flashback         Conflict or  again    Resolution
                       challenge
          Setting  Intro to
                   characters
```

A story might start years later and then the plot continues through a series of flashbacks which increase in intensity.

```
                                    Flashback 3
                    Flashback 2
    Flashback 1

Present                                         Present
```

There are many ways authors construct their narratives. There is space for you to draw and annotate the story arc for each story.

Story 1

Title: _____

Author: _____

What is your immediate **reaction** to this story? Thoughts, feelings, impressions? Anything that impresses or confuses you?

Try to draw and annotate the *story arc*
(For more information, see page 9.)

12 Story 1

What is the **author**'s historical/ cultural context?
Where and when is the **story** set? Does this information impact your understanding of the story?

Story 1

What are the story's main **themes?**
How do you know this? What clues are there in the writing?

Is the author trying to make any **point** in the story?
What might it be?

Story 1

Who are the main *characters?*

Describe them a little. Do they change during the story? What is your opinion of them and their actions?

Story 1

characters? (continued)

Is there a *quote* from the story which tells us something important about how each character thinks or feels (not what they do)?

Story 1

Is there anything **unusual/surprising** about this story? What is it?

Is there a **turning point** in the plot? When?

Is the **ending** satisfying?
Does it resolve/ end the way you expected? Explain why/ why not.

Story 1

What is the *language* of the story like?

Formal/ informal? Is there much dialogue?
In what kind of language do the characters express themselves?
Is there anything surprising or unusual about it?

Story 1

How would you describe the
mood/ tone/ atmosphere
of the story? Select some quotes to illustrate this.

Story 1

Write out *quotes* you think are significant because they illustrate something interesting about the author's ideas, the language used, or a character's development.

Remembering them in the exam could be helpful, so only pick short, really useful ones.

Story 1

Imagine you are writing exam *essay questions* for someone else.

Remember that such questions never ask **what** the plot is. It is assumed that candidates will know what happened in the story. Questions are often about **how** the author has done something.

Write the titles of the *homework* assignments or essays you have been given, or have chosen to work on.

Title	Date:	Due	Completed

Story 1

Story 2

Title: _____

Author: _____

What is your immediate *reaction* to this story? Thoughts, feelings, impressions? Anything that impresses or confuses you?

Try to draw and annotate the *story arc*

Story 2

What is the **author**'s historical/ cultural context?
Where and when is the **story** set? Does this information impact your understanding of the story?

Story 2

What are the story's main **themes?**
How do you know this? What clues are there in the writing?

Is the author trying to make any **point** in the story?
What might it be?

Story 2

Who are the main *characters?*

Describe them a little. Do they change during the story? What is your opinion of them and their actions?

Story 2

characters? (continued)

Is there a *quote* from the story which tells us something important about how each character thinks or feels (not what they do)?

Story 2

Is there anything **unusual/surprising** about this story? What is it?

Is there a **turning point** in the plot? When?

Is the **ending** satisfying? Does it resolve/ end the way you expected? Explain why/ why not.

Story 2

What is the *language* of the story like?

Formal/ informal? Is there much dialogue?
In what kind of language do the characters express themselves?
Is there anything surprising or unusual about it?

Story 2

How would you describe the
mood/ tone/ atmosphere
of the story? Select some quotes to illustrate this.

Story 2

Write out *quotes* you think are significant because they illustrate something interesting about the author's ideas, the language used, or a character's development.

Remembering them in the exam could be helpful, so only pick short, really useful ones.

Story 2

Imagine you are writing exam

essay questions for someone else.

Remember that such questions never ask **what** the plot is. It is assumed that candidates will know what happened in the story. Questions are often about **how** the author has done something.

Write the titles of the **homework** assignments or essays you have been given, or have chosen to work on.

Title	Date:	Due	Completed

Story 2

Story 3

Title: _____

Author: _____

What is your immediate reaction to this story? Thoughts, feelings, impressions? Anything that impresses or confuses you?

Try to draw and annotate the *story arc*

What is the **author**'s historical/ cultural context?
Where and when is the **story** set? Does this information impact your understanding of the story?

Story 3

What are the story's main themes?
How do you know this? What clues are there in the writing?

Is the author trying to make any point in the story?
What might it be?

Story 3

Who are the main *characters?*

Describe them a little. Do they change during the story? What is your opinion of them and their actions?

Story 3

characters? (continued)

Is there a *quote* from the story which tells us something important about how each character thinks or feels (not what they do)?

Story 3

Is there anything **unusual/surprising** about this story? What is it?

Is there a **turning point** in the plot? When?

Is the **ending** satisfying?
Does it resolve/ end the way you expected? Explain why/ why not.

Story 3

What is the *language* of the story like?

Formal/ informal? Is there much dialogue?
In what kind of language do the characters express themselves?
Is there anything surprising or unusual about it?

Story 3

How would you describe the
mood/ tone/ atmosphere
of the story? Select some quotes to illustrate this.

Story 3

Write out *quotes* you think are significant because they illustrate something interesting about the author's ideas, the language used, or a character's development.

Remembering them in the exam could be helpful, so only pick short, really useful ones.

Story 3

Imagine you are writing exam *essay questions* for someone else.

Remember that such questions never ask **what** the plot is. It is assumed that candidates will know what happened in the story. Questions are often about **how** the author has done something.

Write the titles of the *homework* assignments or essays you have been given, or have chosen to work on.

Title	Date:	Due	Completed

Story 3

Story 4

Title:

Author:

What is your immediate *reaction* to this story? Thoughts, feelings, impressions? Anything that impresses or confuses you?

Try to draw and annotate the *story arc*

Story 4

What is the **author**'s historical/ cultural context?
Where and when is the **story** set? Does this information impact your understanding of the story?

Story 4

55

What are the story's main **themes?**
How do you know this? What clues are there in the writing?

Is the author trying to make any **point** in the story?
What might it be?

Story 4

Who are the main *characters?*
Describe them a little. Do they change during the story? What is your opinion of them and their actions?

Story 4

characters? (continued)

Story 4

Is there a *quote* from the story which tells us something important about how each character thinks or feels (not what they do)?

Story 4

Is there anything **unusual/surprising** about this story? What is it?

Is there a **turning point** in the plot? When?

Is the **ending** satisfying?
Does it resolve/ end the way you expected? Explain why/ why not.

Story 4

What is the *language* of the story like?

Formal/ informal? Is there much dialogue?
In what kind of language do the characters express themselves?
Is there anything surprising or unusual about it?

Story 4

How would you describe the
mood/ tone/ atmosphere
of the story? Select some quotes to illustrate this.

Story 4

Write out *quotes* you think are significant because they illustrate something interesting about the author's ideas, the language used, or a character's development.

Remembering them in the exam could be helpful, so only pick short, really useful ones.

Story 4

Imagine you are writing exam *essay questions* for someone else.

Remember that such questions never ask **what** the plot is. It is assumed that candidates will know what happened in the story. Questions are often about **how** the author has done something.

Story 4

Write the titles of the *homework* assignments or essays you have been given, or have chosen to work on.

Title	Date:	Due	Completed

Story 4

Story 5

Title:

Author:

What is your immediate **reaction** to this story? Thoughts, feelings, impressions? Anything that impresses or confuses you?

Try to draw and annotate the *story arc*

What is the **author**'s historical/ cultural context?
Where and when is the **story** set? Does this information impact your understanding of the story?

Story 5

69

What are the story's main **themes?**
How do you know this? What clues are there in the writing?

Is the author trying to make any **point** in the story?
What might it be?

Story 5

Who are the main *characters?*
Describe them a little. Do they change during the story? What is your opinion of them and their actions?

Story 5

characters? (continued)

Is there a *quote* from the story which tells us something important about how each character thinks or feels (not what they do)?

Story 5

Is there anything **unusual/surprising** about this story? What is it?

Is there a **turning point** in the plot? When?

Is the **ending** satisfying? Does it resolve/ end the way you expected? Explain why/ why not.

Story 5

What is the *language* of the story like?

Formal/ informal? Is there much dialogue?
In what kind of language do the characters express themselves?
Is there anything surprising or unusual about it?

Story 5

How would you describe the
mood/ tone/ atmosphere
of the story? Select some quotes to illustrate this.

Write out *quotes* you think are significant because they illustrate something interesting about the author's ideas, the language used, or a character's development.

Remembering them in the exam could be helpful, so only pick short, really useful ones.

Story 5

Imagine you are writing exam *essay questions* for someone else.

Remember that such questions never ask **what** the plot is. It is assumed that candidates will know what happened in the story. Questions are often about **how** the author has done something.

Write the titles of the **homework** assignments or essays you have been given, or have chosen to work on.

Title	Date:	Due	Completed

Story 5

Story 6

Title:

Author:

What is your immediate reaction to this story? Thoughts, feelings, impressions? Anything that impresses or confuses you?

Try to draw and annotate the *story arc*

Story 6

What is the **author**'s historical/ cultural context?
Where and when is the **story** set? Does this information impact your understanding of the story?

Story 6

What are the story's main **themes?**
How do you know this? What clues are there in the writing?

Is the author trying to make any **point** in the story?
What might it be?

Story 6

Who are the main *characters?*

Describe them a little. Do they change during the story? What is your opinion of them and their actions?

Story 6

characters? (continued)

Is there a *quote* from the story which tells us something important about how each character thinks or feels (not what they do)?

Story 6

Is there anything **unusual/surprising** about this story? What is it?

Is there a **turning point** in the plot? When?

Is the **ending** satisfying? Does it resolve/ end the way you expected? Explain why/ why not.

Story 6

What is the *language* of the story like?

Formal/ informal? Is there much dialogue?
In what kind of language do the characters express themselves?
Is there anything surprising or unusual about it?

Story 6

How would you describe the
mood/ tone/ atmosphere
of the story? Select some quotes to illustrate this.

Story 6

Write out *quotes* you think are significant because they illustrate something interesting about the author's ideas, the language used, or a character's development.

Remembering them in the exam could be helpful, so only pick short, really useful ones.

Story 6

Imagine you are writing exam *essay questions* for someone else.

Remember that such questions never ask **what** the plot is. It is assumed that candidates will know what happened in the story. Questions are often about **how** the author has done something.

Write the titles of the **homework** assignments or essays you have been given, or have chosen to work on.

Title	Date:	Due	Completed

Story 6

Story 7

Title: _____
_____

Author: _____

What is your immediate *reaction* to this story? Thoughts, feelings, impressions? Anything that impresses or confuses you?

Try to draw and annotate the *story arc*

Story 7

What is the **author**'s historical/ cultural *context?*
Where and when is the **story** set? Does this information impact your understanding of the story?

Story 1

What are the story's main **themes?**
How do you know this? What clues are there in the writing?

Is the author trying to make any **point** in the story?
What might it be?

Who are the main *characters?*

Describe them a little. Do they change during the story? What is your opinion of them and their actions?

Story 7

characters? (continued)

Story 7

Is there a *quote* from the story which tells us something important about how each character thinks or feels (not what they do)?

Story 7

Is there anything **unusual/surprising** about this story? What is it?

Is there a **turning point** in the plot? When?

Is the **ending** satisfying? Does it resolve/ end the way you expected? Explain why/ why not.

Story 7

What is the *language* of the story like?

Formal/ informal? Is there much dialogue?
In what kind of language do the characters express themselves?
Is there anything surprising or unusual about it?

Story 7

How would you describe the
mood/ tone/ atmosphere
of the story? Select some quotes to illustrate this.

Write out *quotes* you think are significant because they illustrate something interesting about the author's ideas, the language used, or a character's development.

Remembering them in the exam could be helpful, so only pick short, really useful ones.

Story 7

Imagine you are writing exam

essay questions for someone else.

Remember that such questions never ask **what** the plot is. It is assumed that candidates will know what happened in the story. Questions are often about **how** the author has done something.

Story 7

Write the titles of the **homework** assignments or essays you have been given, or have chosen to work on.

Title	Date:	Due	Completed

Story 7

Story 8

Title:

Author:

What is your immediate reaction to this story? Thoughts, feelings, impressions? Anything that impresses or confuses you?

Try to draw and annotate the *story arc*

What is the **author**'s historical/ cultural context?
Where and when is the **story** set? Does this information impact your understanding of the story?

Story 8

111

What are the story's main **themes?**
How do you know this? What clues are there in the writing?

Is the author trying to make any **point** in the story?
What might it be?

Story 8

Who are the main *characters?*

Describe them a little. Do they change during the story? What is your opinion of them and their actions?

characters? (continued)

Is there a *quote* from the story which tells us something important about how each character thinks or feels (not what they do)?

Story 8

Is there anything **unusual/surprising** about this story? What is it?

Is there a **turning point** in the plot? When?

Is the **ending** satisfying? Does it resolve/ end the way you expected? Explain why/ why not.

Story 8

What is the *language* of the story like?

Formal/ informal? Is there much dialogue?
In what kind of language do the characters express themselves?
Is there anything surprising or unusual about it?

Story 8

How would you describe the
mood/ tone/ atmosphere
of the story? Select some quotes to illustrate this.

Write out *quotes* you think are significant because they illustrate something interesting about the author's ideas, the language used, or a character's development.

Remembering them in the exam could be helpful, so only pick short, really useful ones.

Story 8

Imagine you are writing exam *essay questions* for someone else.

Remember that such questions never ask **what** the plot is. It is assumed that candidates will know what happened in the story. Questions are often about **how** the author has done something.

Write the titles of the *homework* assignments or essays you have been given, or have chosen to work on.

Title	Date:	Due	Completed

Story 8

Story 9

Title:

Author:

What is your immediate *reaction* to this story? Thoughts, feelings, impressions? Anything that impresses or confuses you?

Try to draw and annotate the *story arc*

What is the **author**'s historical/ cultural *context?*
Where and when is the **story** set? Does this information impact your understanding of the story?

Story 9

What are the story's main *themes?*
How do you know this? What clues are there in the writing?

Is the author trying to make any *point* in the story?
What might it be?

Story 9

Who are the main *characters?*

Describe them a little. Do they change during the story? What is your opinion of them and their actions?

Story 9

characters? (continued)

Is there a *quote* from the story which tells us something important about how each character thinks or feels (not what they do)?

Story 9

Is there anything **unusual/surprising** about this story? What is it?

Is there a **turning point** in the plot? When?

Is the **ending** satisfying? Does it resolve/ end the way you expected? Explain why/ why not.

Story 9

What is the *language* of the story like?

Formal/ informal? Is there much dialogue?
In what kind of language do the characters express themselves?
Is there anything surprising or unusual about it?

Story 9

How would you describe the
mood/ tone/ atmosphere
of the story? Select some quotes to illustrate this.

Story 9

Write out *quotes* you think are significant because they illustrate something interesting about the author's ideas, the language used, or a character's development.

Remembering them in the exam could be helpful, so only pick short, really useful ones.

Story 9

Imagine you are writing exam

essay questions for someone else.

Remember that such questions never ask **what** the plot is. It is assumed that candidates will know what happened in the story. Questions are often about **how** the author has done something.

Story 9

Write the titles of the **homework** assignments or essays you have been given, or have chosen to work on.

Title	Date:	Due	Completed

Story 9

Story 10

Title: _____
_____

Author: _____

What is your immediate *reaction* to this story? Thoughts, feelings, impressions? Anything that impresses or confuses you?

Try to draw and annotate the *story arc*

What is the **author**'s historical/ cultural context?
Where and when is the **story** set? Does this information impact your understanding of the story?

Story 10   139

What are the story's main **themes?**
How do you know this? What clues are there in the writing?

Is the author trying to make any **point** in the story?
What might it be?

Story 10

Who are the main *characters?*

Describe them a little. Do they change during the story? What is your opinion of them and their actions?

Story 10

characters? (continued)

Is there a *quote* from the story which tells us something important about how each character thinks or feels (not what they do)?

Story 10

Is there anything **unusual/surprising** about this story? What is it?

Is there a **turning point** in the plot? When?

Is the **ending** satisfying?
Does it resolve/ end the way you expected? Explain why/ why not.

Story 10

What is the *language* of the story like?

Formal/ informal? Is there much dialogue?
In what kind of language do the characters express themselves?
Is there anything surprising or unusual about it?

Story 10

How would you describe the
mood/ tone/ atmosphere
of the story? Select some quotes to illustrate this.

Write out **quotes** you think are significant because they illustrate something interesting about the author's ideas, the language used, or a character's development.

Remembering them in the exam could be helpful, so only pick short, really useful ones.

Story 10

Imagine you are writing exam *essay questions* for someone else.

Remember that such questions never ask **what** the plot is. It is assumed that candidates will know what happened in the story. Questions are often about **how** the author has done something.

Story 10

Write the titles of the **homework** assignments or essays you have been given, or have chosen to work on.

Title	Date:	Due	Completed

Story 10

About the author

Photo © Jamie Stewart

Dorothy Murphy is a teacher of English, a mother who home educated her children and a grandmother.

For the last decade or so, she has been helping to prepare home educated teenagers for English Language and Literature International GCSE exams in the UK.

In 2019, she published *Home Education – My First Year*, a guided journal for those parents who are new to home education.

She also wrote a companion book to this one: *Poetry Study Journal for GCSE/ International GCSE English Literature - A place to record your ideas and observations*.

All her books are available through Amazon.

Printed in Great Britain
by Amazon